FITCHBURG PUBLIC LIBRARY
DISCARDED

W9-AUL-637

WILD AMERICA
HABITATS

RAIN FORESTS

By Melissa Cole

BLACKBIRCH®
PRESS

San Diego • Detroit • New York • San Francisco • Cleveland • New Haven, Conn. • Waterville, Maine • London • Munich

THOMSON

GALE

© 2003 by Blackbirch Press™. Blackbirch Press™ is an imprint of The Gale Group, Inc., a division of Thomson Learning, Inc.

Blackbirch Press™ and Thomson Learning™ are trademarks used herein under license.

For more information, contact
The Gale Group, Inc.
27500 Drake Rd.
Farmington Hills, MI 48331-3535
Or you can visit our Internet site at http://www.gale.com

ALL RIGHTS RESERVED
No part of this work covered by the copyright hereon may be reproduced or used in any form or by any means—graphic, electronic, or mechanical, including photocopying, recording, taping, Web distribution, or information storage retrieval systems—without the written permission of the publisher.

Every effort has been made to trace the owners of copyrighted material.

Photo Credits: Cover, all photos © Tom and Pat Leeson Wildlife Photography

LIBRARY OF CONGRESS CATALOGING-IN-PUBLICATION DATA

Cole, Melissa S.
  Rain forests / by Melissa S. Cole.
    v. cm. — (Wild America habitats)
  Contents: Climate — Plants — Animals — Humans and temperate rain forests.
  ISBN 1-56711-808-9 (hardback : alk. paper)
  1. Rain forest ecology—Juvenile literature. [1. Rain forests. 2. Rain forest ecology. 3. Ecology.] I. Title. II. Wild America habitats series.

QH541.5.R27 C65 2003
577.34—dc21   2002013164

Printed in China
10 9 8 7 6 5 4 3 2 1

Contents

Thick clouds often gather above temperate rain forests.

Introduction

Temperate rain forests are one of many types of unique habitats found in North America. Habitats are a specific kind of environment in which only certain plants and animals can survive. There is more living matter in temperate rain forests than in any other habitat on earth—including tropical rain forests.

The climate in temperate rain forests is very wet. Thick gray clouds often hang in the sky above rain forests and ocean fog rolls in through the trees. Water drips from mossy branches. Trees thrive in this kind of weather. On the forest floor, dense layers of pine needles and rotting wood hold moisture in like a sponge. This keeps tree roots damp—even during dry summers.

North America contains the largest continuous area of coastal temperate rain forest in the world. Rain forests stretch from Kodiak Island in southern Alaska to Oregon. They even reach parts of California's redwood forests.

What Makes Rain Forests Unique?

The climate in temperate rain forests is mild, or temperate. In North America, coastal mountains protect these forests from severe weather and create a mild climate there. It is wet and cool. This type of climate occurs where ocean air hits coastal mountains. These conditions cause large amounts of rain to fall. Rainfall in temperate rain forests ranges from 140 to 170 inches (356 to 432 cm) per year. Storms can drop up to 6 inches (15 cm) of rain in 24 hours.

It is almost always cloudy in temperate rain forests. Clouds act like a blanket. They keep temperatures warm in winter and cool in summer. The temperature seldom drops below freezing (32°F/0°C) during winter months, and summer temperatures rarely climb above 80°F (27°C).

Opposite: Mountains along the coast protect rain forests from extreme weather conditions. **Inset:** The fall season in temperate rain forests is cool and wet.

Layers of Plants in Rain Forests

Plants thrive in the mild, moist conditions of the temperate rain forest. Different types of plants live in certain layers of the forest. Where they live is determined by how much light, moisture, and nutrients they need to survive.

Evergreen trees dominate the top layer of the rain forest. This is called the canopy. This layer receives the most sunlight. A few big-leaf maples grow tall enough to become part of the canopy as well. The tallest trees are able to absorb the greatest amount of sunlight. Tops of evergreen trees in the canopy can grow to be up to 300 feet (91 m) tall, measure 60 feet (18 m) around, and live for more than 1,000 years.

The canopy gets the most sunlight because it is the highest layer of plants in a rain forest.

Other plants such as club moss, Spanish moss, licorice ferns, and lichens grow on tree branches that are more than 250 feet (76 m) high. There, they can soak up sunlight that shines in the upper layers of the forest. These plants are called epiphytes. They hang like curtains from tall trees. This gives the rain forest its jungle-like appearance. Sunlight is important to all rainforest vegetation, but only the top layers receive it regularly.

Moss and licorice ferns grow on high tree branches in rain forests.

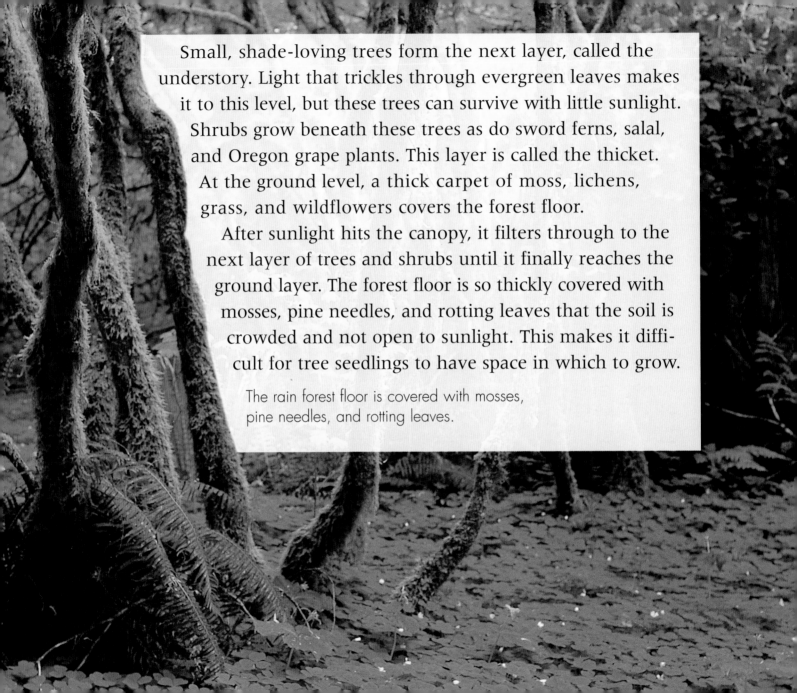

Small, shade-loving trees form the next layer, called the understory. Light that trickles through evergreen leaves makes it to this level, but these trees can survive with little sunlight. Shrubs grow beneath these trees as do sword ferns, salal, and Oregon grape plants. This layer is called the thicket. At the ground level, a thick carpet of moss, lichens, grass, and wildflowers covers the forest floor.

After sunlight hits the canopy, it filters through to the next layer of trees and shrubs until it finally reaches the ground layer. The forest floor is so thickly covered with mosses, pine needles, and rotting leaves that the soil is crowded and not open to sunlight. This makes it difficult for tree seedlings to have space in which to grow.

The rain forest floor is covered with mosses, pine needles, and rotting leaves.

Rotting needles and leaves are broken down in the soil and make it rich with nutrients. A fallen, rotting log is an ideal place for tree seedlings to sprout. As fallen logs—known as nurse logs—decay, they provide nutrients needed for seedlings to grow. They grow in a straight line along the nurse log. This is called a colonnade. Eventually the nurse log rots away and leaves the giant trees standing on stilt-like roots.

Because very little light makes it to the forest floor, many wildflowers have a short growing season. They bloom and set seed in early March. This is before overhead leaves in the canopy layer open and block most of the sunlight.

Tree seedlings grow in fallen logs called nurse logs.

About 350 species of birds and animals live in the temperate rain forest. Some animals develop special adaptations to live in this habitat. For example, flying squirrels have web-like skin that stretches along their sides from their front legs to their rear legs. When they spread their four legs apart, the extra skin fans out and forms a kind of wing on each side of their bodies. This allows them to glide through the air between branches.

Pileated woodpeckers are one of many species of woodpeckers in temperate rain forests. They are large birds with brilliant red crests on the tops of their heads. They dig holes in trees to make nests for their young. They feed on insects that live under the thick layers of bark by hammering into it with their strong beaks. Woodpeckers have thick skulls to help cushion their brains from the constant pounding.

Pileated woodpeckers use their beaks to hammer holes into trees. Then, they feed on insects that live underneath the bark.

They have sharp beaks and long tongues, which allow them to scoop insects out from below the bark.

Beavers also live in the rain forest. They feed on the juicy layer of wood found below the surface of a tree's bark. They can gnaw down a tree that is over 3 feet (1 m) in diameter. They build dens or tunnels along the sides of streams. Other small animals live here, too. Raccoons, porcupines, and pine martens (weasel-like creatures) sleep in the crooks of trees. They feed on plants, bird eggs, insects, fish, and frogs.

Beavers gnaw on tree branches to eat the wood beneath the bark.

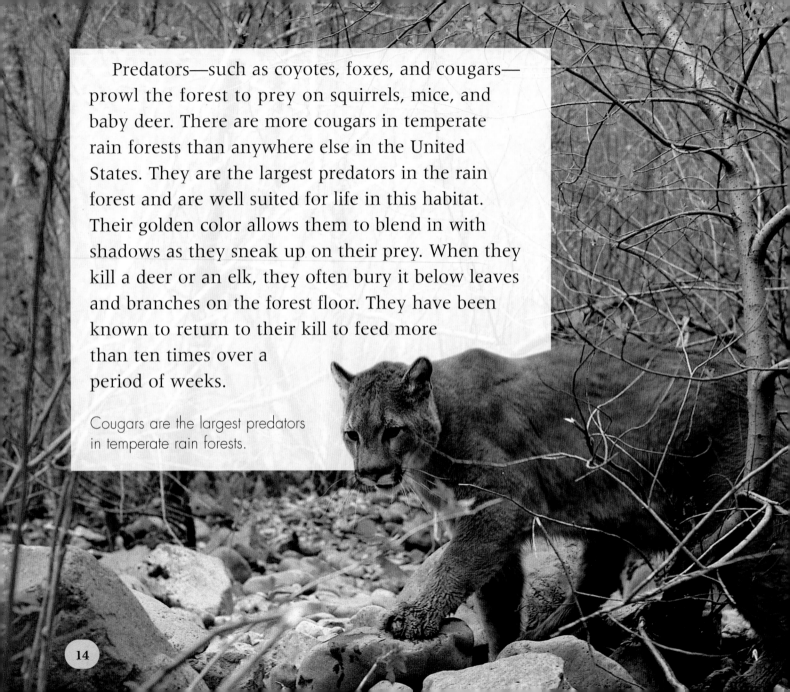

Predators—such as coyotes, foxes, and cougars—prowl the forest to prey on squirrels, mice, and baby deer. There are more cougars in temperate rain forests than anywhere else in the United States. They are the largest predators in the rain forest and are well suited for life in this habitat. Their golden color allows them to blend in with shadows as they sneak up on their prey. When they kill a deer or an elk, they often bury it below leaves and branches on the forest floor. They have been known to return to their kill to feed more than ten times over a period of weeks.

Cougars are the largest predators in temperate rain forests.

Most prey, such as black-tailed deer fawns, are born in spring. Their coats are light brown with white spots. This allows them to blend in with shadow and light patterns on the forest floor. During their first few weeks of life, they spend much of their time lying still so they are not noticed by predators.

Roosevelt elk are particularly well adapted to rainforest life because they have narrow antlers. The size of their antlers allows them to move easily through dense forest and underbrush. Male elk develop new antlers each summer. Each winter their antlers fall off. Many rainforest animals chew on discarded antlers in order to get minerals such as calcium and potassium.

Above: Black-tailed deer fawns lie still to avoid being noticed by predators. **Right:** Roosevelt elk have narrow antlers, a feature that allows them to move easily through dense rain forests.

On the Floor and in the Water

Each spring and fall, salmon migrate from the ocean to the same rivers and streams where they were born. They travel hundreds of miles to lay their eggs, to spawn (to produce young in large numbers), and to die. Salmon are an important food source for many animals. Black bears, bald eagles, river otters, and mink come to the river in spring to search for these tasty, high-protein fish.

Salmon travel hundreds of miles each spring and fall to spawn in the rivers and streams where they were born.

Other animals live on the soggy forest floor. Salamanders, frogs, and banana slugs need to keep their skin moist. Damp moss on the bottoms of trees provides a comfortable place for these creatures. When the weather is hot and dry, these animals hide under wet leaves and rotting logs. This keeps them cool and moist.

Banana slugs live on the damp rainforest floor.

Fungi grow along rotting trees on the forest floor.

Food Chain

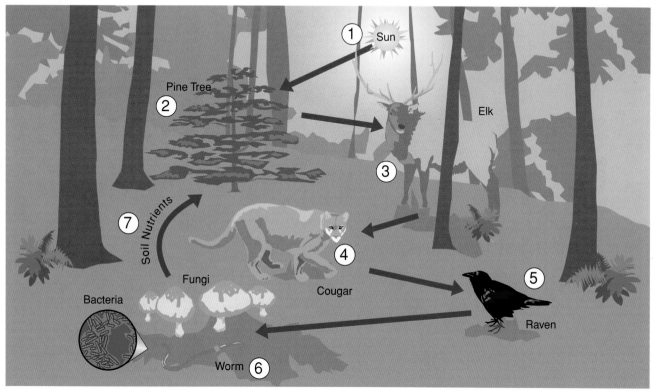

The food chain shows a step-by-step example of how energy in the rainforest habitat is exchanged through food: The sun (1) is the first source of energy for all living things on earth. Green plants such as grasses, shrubs, and trees (2) are able to use sunlight and carbon dioxide in the air to create sugar, which the plants use as food. An elk (3) might eat the new shoots on the pine tree for food. Then, the elk becomes the prey of a cougar (4). When the cougar dies, ravens (5) and other scavengers feed on its dead body. When a raven dies, worms, fungi, bacteria (6), and other decomposers feed on its body. Finally, these creatures or their waste products end up as soil nutrients (7), which are then taken up by the roots of the pine trees as part of their nourishment. The cycle then repeats.

Humans and Rain Forests

People called homesteaders settled the rain forest in the 1890s. Many acres of trees were cut down, or logged, to clear land for farms. Today, more than 90 percent of the ancient rain forest has been logged because of a high demand for lumber and paper products.

Though logging has been part of the rain forest for hundreds of years, spot clearing (when a few trees are cut down in different areas) is becoming more widespread. This type of logging helps to prevent soil erosion. Soil erosion occurs when topsoil is no longer held in place by the roots of plants and trees. When this happens, the rich top layer of soil washes into streams when it rains. Once the soil washes away, it is almost impossible for the habitat to recover.

Logging rain forests for wood can cause soil erosion.

Although parks and reserves have been set aside, many animals are endangered. This is because it is difficult for them to survive in the small patches of forest that remain.

Rivers near rain forests are often dammed to produce electrical power and to provide water to farmlands. Dams can flood thousands of acres of land and kill many plants and animals. Dams also change the flow of rivers and streams. This disrupts the migration of salmon and other animals.

Spotted owls often live in old trees that grow in temperate rain forests.

There are many ways people can preserve rain forests. Environmental groups try to convince logging companies to leave logged forests alone so trees have a chance to grow old. People who buy recycled paper products reduce the need for paper and help save trees. Recycling glass, cans, and paper also conserves many natural resources. Another way to help the environment is to use cloth shopping bags, towels, diapers, and napkins instead of paper ones. This also reduces the need for paper, slows down logging, and allows rain forests to recover.

A Rain Forest's Food Web

A food web shows how creatures in a habitat depend on one another to survive. The arrows in this drawing show the flow of energy from one creature to another. Yellow arrows: creatures nourished by the sun; Green arrows: animals that eat green plants; Orange arrows: predators; Red arrows: scavengers and decomposers. Whatever is left becomes part of the soil and is taken up by green plants as part of their nourishment, and the cycle repeats.

Glossary

Adaptation A change in the behavior or characteristics of a plant or animal that increases its chances of survival in a particular habitat

Habitat The area in which a plant or animal naturally lives. Habitat provides living organisms with everything they need to survive—food, water, and shelter.

Lichen A type of organism formed by fungi and algae living together in a partnership

For Further Reading

Books

Lewington, Anna. *Atlas of Rainforests.* Houston: Raintree Steck-Vaughn Publishers, 1997.

Martin, Patricia. *Woods and Forests.* New York: Grolier Publishing, 2000.

Wright-Frierson, Virginia. *A North American Rainforest Scrapbook.* New York: Walker and Co., 1999.

Web sites

Olympic Rainforest site
http://www.youra.com/olympic/rainforest.html

Index